Carlos the Jackal: The Life of the 20th Century's Most Notorious Terrorist

By Charles River Editors

About Charles River Editors

Charles River Editors provides superior editing and original writing services across the digital publishing industry, with the expertise to create digital content for publishers across a vast range of subject matter. In addition to providing original digital content for third party publishers, we also republish civilization's greatest literary works, bringing them to new generations of readers via ebooks.

Sign up here to receive updates about free books as we publish them, and visit Our Kindle Author Page to browse today's free promotions and our most recently published Kindle titles.

Introduction

Carlos the Jackal (1949-)

The history of terrorism as a self-appointed profession can be traced back to the dawn of the human community, and each era claims its own class of celebrities. However, it was in the 20th century in which individual terrorists first gained access to the type of advanced weaponry that could cause mass killings and destroy major public institutions. In the modern age, entire communities and countries can be held hostage to demands based upon the threat of personal or state violence, and playing upon mankind's greatest fears has risen to a new level of creativity as cultures, religions, and governmental ideologies square off in an ever-shrinking globe.

From the early 1970s through the following two decades, the cult star of worldwide terrorism was Ilich Ramirez Sanchez of Venezuela, better known to the world as Carlos the Jackal. Sanchez, the most notorious of terrorists in the late 20th century before Osama bin Laden's destructive 9/11 attacks, was born on October 12, 1949, in the years following the most global example of state terrorism in the form of Nazi Germany. Sanchez was known to virtually every European and American who read the news between 1970 and 1990, but it was his moniker, Carlos the Jackal, that signified his status as a household word.

During Sanchez' reign as what has been called, "the first super terrorist,"[1] the world found it unthinkable that any future attack on society could outdo his spectacular raids on Western

---

[1] Rotten.com – Carlos the Jackal – www.rotten.com/library/bio/crime/terrorists/carlos-the-jackal/

targets, specifically European ones. For young generations growing up in the 21st century, the operative code-named Carlos may have slipped into distant history, but as one put it, "Before there was Osama bin Laden…before there was Ramzi Yousef, there was the jackal."[2]

Carlos the Jackal: The Life of the 20th Century's Most Notorious Terrorist looks at the violent life and legacy of the Jackal. Along with pictures of important people, places, and events, you will learn about Carlos the Jackal like never before, in no time at all.

---

[2] Rotten.com – Carlos the Jackal

Carlos the Jackal: The Life of the 20th Century's Most Notorious Terrorist

About Charles River Editors

Introduction

Chapter 1: Early Years

Ilich Ramirez Sanchez

Born in Michilena, young Ilich Ramirez Sanchez was raised firmly under the influence of his father, Jose Altagracia Ramirez Navas, a man whose life provided a study in contrasts, to say the least. A devout Marxist to the point of fanaticism, Navas had once considered the Catholic priesthood as a potential vocation, but in the end went into the practice of law, at one time working as a property developer as well. The priesthood and living as a land baron was an interesting choice for a devoted Marxist who believed in equal distribution of wealth. Despite his activism for the Marxist cause, however, he seemed able to reconcile the existence of his personal fortune with his ideological beliefs, and was dubbed by sources close to him as the "Millionaire Marxist." [3]

Sanchez' mother, Ella Maria Sanchez, was born in the Venezuelan state of Tachira and was raised a devout Catholic, despite leanings toward living as a socialite in the Caracas community. Urging her son to follow the church, her influence on his future was always superseded by her husband's rigidity, and the children were named after the most high-profile Russian revolutionaries that instituted the birth of the Soviet Union in the early 20th century. Despite the differences between Marxist, Leninist, and Stalinist forms of communism, Navas embraced them uniformly, and set his son on an educational path that at all times emphasized a leftist philosophy. Rather than a formal education based only in the Venezuelan capital city, Navas made sure that his son's training was an international one, with studies at Stafford House College of Canterbury for part of his high school years. Although his parents divorced in 1962, when he was 13, Carlos continued in this ideological vein at the Tora Lycee School, up to the age of 15.

---

[3] Rotten.com – Carlos the Jackal

His father's hopes were, in time, borne out as his son offered a full commitment to the Venezuelan Communist Party, joining their membership shortly out of school in 1964. Furthering his European education, Sanchez went on to study at the University of London and at Central London Polytechnic. There, he branched out from strictly ideological teachings to practical technological information that was to become central to his later vocation. In January of 1966, at the age of 17, he participated in Camp Matanzas, a "guerilla warfare school" held in Cuba and run by the Cuban DGI, again at the urging of his father. In the same year, he attended the Third Tricontinental Congress held in Havana for the political promotion of African, Asian, and Latin American Peoples. For the young Sanchez, the Congress was a festival for the mind as 83 Marxist and anti-Imperialist groups attended, including the Soviet Union with 40 delegates, most of Asia with 177, and the African continent, represented by 150. The central tone of the Congress was vociferously pro-Castro, and thus was not held in Havana by accident. Entirely at one with his father's position, Sanchez continued his training in weaponry at a Jordanian camp, experiencing life in the Middle East for the first time. Such international influences were well-suited for the young Marxist, as he was gifted in as many as seven languages from a young age, a skill that helped him find his way around the world with ease in later years.

Castro

In one last attempt to regain some control over her son's future, Sanchez' mother tried to help him enroll in the Sorbonne, where he might receive a more classical education and distance himself somewhat from the intensity of the Marxist movement in which he was raised. This effort failing, however, Sanchez ended up instead at the Patrice Lumumba University in Moscow, in the heart of Soviet Russia. Named for a revered Congolese independence leader, the university sat as a jewel in Russia's academic crown, and symbolized the cultivation of all things Soviet. Numerous young people who would go on to become government officials attended, and as a general policy, full scholarships were offered to all. The approximately 6,500 foreign students represented 70% of the student body, and it was Moscow's intent that such students return to their home countries with a distinctly Soviet bent. After the eventual fall of the Soviet Union, the university disintegrated through the years into a distinctly second class institution and shadow of its former self, described by one Western publication as Moscow's "academic nightmare." [4]

Lumumba

Lamentably for Sanchez, he was not to call Lumumba his alma mater, being expelled in 1970 for what the institution labeled as his penchant for "leading a life of dissipation."[5]

---

[4] Clara Germani, The Baltimore Sun, Nov. 5, 1995 – www.articles.baltimoresun.com/1995-11-05/news/1995309007_1_patricia -lumumba-university-dream-school-moscow

Chapter 2: New Perspectives

The time Sanchez spent in Moscow did not go entirely to waste, however. It was during this period that he developed a fascination with the political welfare of Palestine, and his Russian tenure became the first opportunity for him to delve into Islam as an area of general interest. His developing involvement with Islam, however, with its strict rules of private and public behavior, came to be increasingly at odds with his "life of dissipation." As his early bent toward anti-imperialist violence began, he acquired a certain "flamboyance"[6] that did not fit in with the dictates of Islamic dogma. Those who knew him from this time were concerned that Sanchez saw himself as living a Bond-like existence, that he was "keenly image conscious"[7] and aspiring to become the world's next "terrorist pinup."[8]

At the age of 21 in 1970, Sanchez joined the Popular Front for the Liberation of Palestine, and began his next phase of guerilla training at a camp in Amman, Jordan. He was recruited for Wadie Haddad– aka Abu Hani – the leader of the military wing of the PFLP, by Bassam Abu Sharif, co-founder of the Arab Nationalist Movement. Haddad, who specialized in the art of hijacking airliners, had met Sanchez earlier in the same year, and it was in Jordan that he received the code name of *Carlos*.

[5] The Guardian, Tuesday, July, 1975 – www.theguardian.com'us-news/2015/jul/08/carlos-the-jackal-in-london-1975

[6] Manohla Dargis, The New York Times, Oct. 2010 – The Days, Nights, and Years of The Jackal: The Tale of a Terrorist – www.nytimes.com/2010/10/15/15carlos.html?_r=0

[7] Manohla Dargis, The New York Times

[8] Manohla Dargis, The New York Times

Haddad

Being of South American origins, Carlos fell into the category of *foreign volunteers*, and as all non-Arab fighters were, he was sent to a training camp for all such individuals until he merited the trust necessary to fight with a passionate and secretive Arab force. Following his time there, Carlos was sent on to what the leadership delicately called a "finishing school,"[9] more officially dubbed H-4. In a striking example of Middle Eastern connectedness that surrounds most major sociological and geographical issues of the region, H-4 was staffed almost entirely by the Iraqi military. This later formed either actual or perceived links between Carlos and Iraqi dictator Saddam Hussein.

---

[9] The New York Times, The Question of Carlos, Review of The Search for Carlos, the World's Most Wanted Man, Random House, New York, Jan. 1994 – www.nytimes.com/1994/01/02/books/the-question-of-Carlos.html

Hussein

Between the years of 1970 and 1973, several sensationalistic events took place, all widely covered in the press, involving terrorist activity against institutions and individuals on the European continent. Carlos' name came up as a possible participant and suspect in all of them, but the extent or nature of his role was not yet clearly discernible.

Meeting with the PFLP in Beirut in 1971, Carlos provided a full-page and straightforward interview for the Omani newspaper *Al Watan al Arabi*, originally intended to be distributed as a daily, but in time, on the stands as a weekly in Beirut. This and other public appearances indicated that Carlos did not fall into the category of a *phantom terrorist*, and he clearly enjoyed the attentions of a world just becoming familiar with his public identity.

In the summer of 1972, a small number of Palestinian operatives climbed over the six-foot cyclone fence into the Olympic Village in Munich. Impersonating athletes, they wore track sweats and carried athletic bags, appearing as team members but concealing a cache of weapons. They were in possession of stolen keys, and managed to avoid being questioned by any security officers along the way. This was not so difficult, as it was somewhat customary for athletes in that part of the village to enter via the fence. A short time later, 11 Israeli athletes lay dead in a massacre, and while Carlos was nowhere to be seen at Munich, it has been theorized that his presence was central to the event. Some have even described him as the "godfather"[10] of the operation, although his responsibility remains difficult to pinpoint.

Unlike previous collaborations and missions, the first public assassination in which Carlos was involved placed him directly in the center as the gunman. Joseph Edward Sieff, a well-known member of the London Jewish community as President of the Marks and Spencer retail store, was chosen as the ideal target for an attack against the center of the Jewish interests in the city. It is believed that the intended assassination of Sieff was planned as retaliation against Israel for its killing of a high-level Palestinian figure in the wake of Munich Olympics massacre.

Sieff, in his late 60s, suspected that he might become a target in the Palestinian conflict, but he would never have imagined that the killer would appear at his home and simply knock on the front door in December of 1973. With no serious attempt at fashioning a disguise, Carlos arrived carrying a 9 mm Beretta pistol for his first official mission as the triggerman. Alternate sources claim that the shooting was done with a 7.62 mm Tokarev, but regardless, when a Portuguese butler answered the door for the Sieff family, Carlos pulled the gun and pointed it at the man's face, then instructed him to lead the way to Sieff, who was preparing for the dinner hour in an upstairs bathroom. Climbing the stairs, Sieff's wife Lois saw the strange guest and the gun he carried being held against the butler's back. Running into her bedroom, she called the police.

Sieff and Carlos faced one another in the upstairs room, and from approximately three feet away, Carlos fired and shot his victim in the head. The shot ricocheted off the thick bone between the bridge of the nose and the eye socket, knocking him unconscious. However, as Carlos prepared to deliver the finishing shot, his pistol jammed, leaving him with no choice but to flee the house. Even at such a short distance, Sieff survived the head wound, leading to speculation among crime analysts and colleagues that throughout Carlos' career, he continually demonstrated poor skills as a marksman.

---

[10] BBC News, World, Carlos the Jackal, Three Decades of Crime – www.news.bbc.co.uk/2/hi/42244.stm

Sieff

Despite his inexperience at the center of such actions, Carlos had gained much trust in the anti-Israeli world for his support and nebulous participation in the Olympic murders and smaller actions. For Europe and the United States, in fact, he became "the template for the western idea of an international terrorist."[11]

1973 saw a number of localized attacks on French institutions, communication centers, and transportation systems, including an assault on the branch of a large Israeli bank in the city of Paris. Carlos was also the mastermind behind several newspaper building bombings that year, although the early part of his career was marked by an inclination to minimize injuries and deaths. In the 1973 attacks, it became Carlos' trademark to announce his intentions in advance and offer "courteous warning calls"[12] to ensure "limited casualties."[13] The destruction of the institution and the upsetting of the victim country's system was the more important symbolic message, not the death toll of various citizens and low to middle officials.

As his missions grew in number, however, and his willingness to kill his victims became more detached and clinical, various Middle Eastern groups took more notice of his European attacks. As national and international police forces around the globe stepped up the search for the increasingly high-profile guerilla fighter, Carlos found refuge and a well of material support in Lebanon, Yemen, Syria, Iraq, and Libya, among others. Such support came in the form of identity protection, an ample supply of weaponry, strong mission financing, and a vast network of safe houses. He was increasingly treated by his hosts as "a specialist,"[14] a member of the elite.

[11] History of War, Ilich Ramirez Sanchez (Carlos the Jackal) 1949 – www.historyofwar.org/articles/people_jackal.html

[12] Rotten.com, Carlos the Jackal – www.rotten.com/library/bio/crime/terrorists/carlos-the-jackal/

[13] Rotten.com, Carlos the Jackal

Chapter 3: The Mid-70s

By the mid-1970s, Carlos had become one of the Cold War's most infamous international criminals in the eyes of the West. Sensing the growing myth around his activities, he embraced his love of flamboyant fashion, romance, and political fantasy, and began to play for bigger stakes in a career described by one biographer as "riddled with bodies, rutted by explosions, and festooned with publicity."[15] The United States, already enamored of the James Bond persona, became fascinated with his exploits, as none of his missions had yet come near American locales or direct interests. While Europe suffered the anxiety of anticipating further attacks, Carlos and the Palestinian/Israeli conflict were "still far enough from American soil for Americans to consider it glamorous."[16]

By 1974, targets had shifted toward government institutions, and Carlos' associations grew more radicalized. With a small group of well-trained members from the Japanese Red Army, an anti-imperialist faction formed in 1970 that split from the Japanese Communist League soon after its inception, Carlos mounted an attack on the French Embassy in The Hague, Netherlands. In this raid, he and his team took captive a group of 10 hostages. The Japanese Red Army consisted of 30-40 members at any given time, each one dedicated to overthrowing the Japanese government and to destroying any international institution that supported the current Japanese regime. As was customary in the majority of cases, demands for the release of hostages were based on the release of imprisoned members from European prisons. Through these bolder raids, Carlos purportedly grew more mercenary, causing a noticeable discomfort among the leaders of the Popular Front for the Liberation of Palestine, whose ideologies required a more secretive and modest lifestyle. Nevertheless, he was considered increasingly useful as well, all while amassing a personal fortune that totaled in the tens of millions.

By January of 1975, Carlos was seen as Wadie Haddad's head man in Paris, having met the leadership of the PFLP some years prior through his "recruiting officer," Bassam Abu Sharif, a close advisor to Yasser Arafat and a co-founder of the Arab Nationalist Movement. It was Sharif who provided Sanchez with the code name of Carlos, and with these alliances, he began to strike directly at Israeli targets, including direct assaults on Israeli airlines at Paris' Orly Airport. His record of triumphs continued to be sketchy at best, however, as he was unable to afflict the anticipated damage with a bombardment of rocket-propelled grenades.

---

[14] Rotten.com, Carlos the Jackal

[15] Manohla Dargis, The New York Times, October, 2010 – The Days, Nights, and Years of the Jackal: The Tale of a Terrorist – www.nytimes.com/2010/10/15/15carlos.html?_r=0

[16] Rotten.com, Carlos the Jackal

Arafat in Lebanon in the 1970s

Much of the remainder of 1975 continued in this "hit and miss" fashion, and several high-profile bombings were entirely bungled through one oversight or another. Among the most pervasive problems Carlos experienced was a regimen of unclear strategies, vague leadership and unreliable funding, leading one biographer to remark in retrospect that his "feats had murky origins…unclear goals and sponsors."[17]

Despite several failures in 1975, it eventually became the year in which Carlos successfully executed two of the boldest and most shocking actions for which he is most vividly remembered. Following so many attempted attacks, he chose to remain in target-rich Paris rather than seek the ever-available haven of various Middle Eastern countries. Such a decision almost spelled the end of his career. In an agreement with the French police, fellow terrorist Michel Moukharbal agreed to lead two counterintelligence agents to Carlos' locale in the Latin Quarter of Paris. The counterintelligence agents made no attempt at a stealthy approach to the apartment, and Carlos actually greeted them at the door and invited all three in for what seemed like an ordinary interview, although he knew too well that they had come to arrest him. He greeted them as if at a

---

[17] About News, Carlos the Jackal – Profile of Carlos the Jackal – www.terrorism.about.com/od/groupsleader/p/CarlostheJackal.htm

planned social event, and even fixed drinks for the three before pulling out a machine pistol and fatally shooting all three. Moukharbal was presumably killed for giving up Carlos' location, and the agents were, by all accounts, unarmed.

Moukharbal

All members of the *Surveille Territoire* were expected to carry pistols for such encounters, and the absence of standard weapons calls into question the real intent of the visit. It is believed that Carlos killed one of the men as he sat drunk at the table. Presumably, an arrest would have taken place immediately upon arrival, but regardless, before local and national law enforcement knew what had happened, he successfully escaped to Beirut by way of Brussels. From there, he rejoined Haddad in the city of Aden, the capital of communist-controlled South Yemen.

By July of that same year, Carlos was thought to be seen in London on numerous occasions after undergoing several major changes in appearance. According to *The Guardian*, he was at that time the subject of an intense manhunt in 12 countries, but in contrast to former times, however, he lacked the customary support from Middle Eastern and European terror groups. A woman who knew Carlos personally was the first to make note of his arrival in Kensington, with his hair cut short, and without his trademark glasses. He was, in the words of authorities who searched for him throughout the country, "friendless, running out of money, and looking for help."[18]

Masterfully keeping one step ahead in maintaining an anonymous identity, British and French

---

[18] The Guardian, Tuesday, July 8, 1975 – www.theguardian.com/us-news/2015/july-08/carlos-the-jackal-in-London-1975

authorities waded through a string of aliases to track him, unsure as to whether they had accounted for all of them. At the time, they were aware of six distinct personas adopted by Carlos, each with an accompanying rap sheet and carrying a falsified passport. During his time in Britain, at his most vulnerable, authorities were still not able to apprehend him. He was last known to stay with friend and supporter, Angela Ortega, before leaving the country. Although Carlos was never caught, Ortega was charged with possession of firearms and ammunition in violation of British law.

After he escaped being caught, the crowning achievement of Carlos' career took place at the end of 1975 in a December raid on a conference at OPEC Headquarters held in the city of Vienna. The Organization of the Petroleum Exporting Countries served as the ideal target with which to express indignation at the manipulation of oil prices by a Middle East at odds with itself. The mastermind behind the design of the attack remained unclear, but it is purported that it was funded by "an Arab president."[19] Some suggested that Saddam Hussein initiated an action in collaboration with the Venezuelan, although Carlos claimed in hindsight that the Iraqi dictator expressed no interest in or recognition of Carlos and his team. Others believe that the raid in Vienna was carried out with the blessing and assistance of Libya's Muammar Gaddafi, the most revered of the Middle Eastern leaders in Carlos' estimation. Still others claim that the operation was funded by the Saudis on behalf of Iran.

---

[19] The Guardian, Tuesday, July 8, 1975

Gaddafi

The team consisting of a handful of operatives reflected the presence of European-born terrorists as much as it did Middle Eastern or Asian operatives. Included in the small group was Gabriele Krocher-Tiedemann and Hans Joachim Klein as cell leaders, befriended at a time when Carlos worked as a chauffeur for Jean-Paul Sartre. Krocher-Tiedemann, the lone female gunman, whose *nom de guerre* was Nada, had killed a policeman attempting to arrest her in 1973 and went on to murder two individuals in the OPEC assault. Klein was a member of the RZ (Revolutionary Cells) and known as Angie in the mission. He later did an about-face and renounced violence. So well-trained were they that it was said that the small group could likely have held off a force many times its size.

Klein

In taking over the OPEC conference, Carlos was responsible for capturing and holding between 60 and 70 hostages, many of them high-ranking diplomatic officials representing several countries. Among his first demands was an airliner to ferry the captives to various spots in several African countries, a request that was granted in short order. In the process of escaping Austria, three officials were killed, including an Austrian policeman, an Iraqi and a Libyan OPEC employee. Carlos himself claims to have killed the Libyan, Yousef Izmirli.

While waiting for the arrival of the airliner, he instructed the Austrian government to broadcast a communiqué at regular intervals over national media outlining the Palestinian cause. Carlos added that if the Austrians refused or delayed, a hostage would be killed every 15 minutes. Thanks to the compliance of the host country, the threatened killings were averted.

After several North African stops, Algiers in particular, Carlos released the non-Jewish hostages, but in the following phase of the operation, which lasted for more than a week, he ran afoul of his pro-Palestinian sponsors on two points. Of greatest importance was that he disobeyed specific instructions to kill both the Saudi Oil Minister and the Iranian Interior Minister. Once the hostages were released, these two, marked for death as a central part of the operation, were set free as well. Second, the masterminds of the raid claimed that Carlos pocketed some or all of the ransom money in the amount of approximately $50 million, and by doing so, utterly betrayed the trust placed in him by the Palestinians. Carlos has always insisted that he stole none of the ransom money because it never arrived; instead, he claimed the ransom was "diverted en route and lost by the revolution."[20] Some sources claim to know where and how such a large cache of funds was "diverted," citing Saddam Hussein as the source and suggesting that Carlos sold out Hussein by sparing the officials and taking $20 million from the Saudis instead to execute the plan to their satisfaction. This hypothesis is somewhat suspect, according to historians, as Hussein later recruited Carlos for specific assassinations as a pretext for killing Saudi opponents, and for making the price of oil rise.

Whatever the case, Carlos reveled in what was ultimately the high point of his career. His attack dominated the opening story of virtually every news broadcast in the world. He was soon to realize, however, that the manner in which he discharged his duties in the eyes of the Palestinians would forever alter his status as a worldwide terrorist attached to an idealistic organization leading the fight for a homeland. On one side, he was hunted with far more intensity than ever before, and by a wider array of authorities from Western states, including the CIA and Interpol. As eluding capture became increasingly difficult, Carlos' safe havens immediately dwindled after the Popular Front for the Liberation of Palestine expelled him from their number following the OPEC raid. Where he had once held the status of a hero, almost a saint, in a multi-national movement, his reputation in the Middle East dictated that future activities be executed as a less scrupulous "gun for hire," suitable for assassinations and the settling of cross-border grudges, not as a freedom fighter for a disenfranchised people.

Chapter 4: The Jackal

Continuing to elude capture along the way, Carlos was seen in various parts of Yugoslavia before being detained there and eventually being flown to Baghdad. He eventually worked his way back to Aden, where he attempted to establish his own Organization of Armed Struggle for the Palestinian cause without the blessing of the PFLP. As French and British law enforcement officers followed his path through a series of safe houses, the nickname of "Jackal" was first associated with Carlos when the John Forsyth novel *Day of the Jackal* was discovered among his possessions. The novel is centered on an assassin's attempts to kill Charles de Gaulle. The moniker caught on with the press, and before long, one name was seldom pronounced without the other.

With European authorities closing in and the Middle East no longer viable outside of individual cloak-and-dagger missions, Carlos' supply of friends and safe zones continued to evaporate. In 1976, however, he was befriended by an unexpected institution: East Germany's Secret Police, the STASI. As a Marxist, he was deemed an asset in the East German state that served as a buffer between the Soviet Union and the West, despite some misgivings about his lifestyle. These concerns, unlike the Palestinian insistence on personal morality, were more matters of discipline and the ability to act secretly, involving Carlos' love of public adulation and the high life. On the other side, as one noted author put it, the Palestinians increasingly

---

[20] Murders and Mysteries, Carlos the Jackal – www.mysteriesandmurders.blogspot.com/2011/07/carlos-the-jackal.html

disavowed him as he began to "revel in the notoriety of his terrorist crime wave."[21] An alarmingly informative interview in Al Watan al Arabi did him no favors with this Palestinian hosts, and served as a rather public statement for one so caught up with retaining anonymity and eluding capture.

Still, the STASI brought Carlos at least partially into the fold, providing him with a number of safe houses in Berlin, securing his telephones, and offering him a car kept in good repair on a *gratis* basis. While Carlos atypically sought to downplay his involvement with the STASI, shredded documents pieced together by law enforcement agencies some time later suggest that the relationship went far beyond what was originally known. Providing him with sanctuary, the STASI also supplied him with an impressive array of weaponry, including not only guns but high explosives and an "archive of forged papers"[22] with which to transport and employ them. To complete the support system that would bring him into full employment with not only the STASI but to a closer connection with the Soviet KGB as well, a list of well-placed accomplices were added to his daily regimen, hailing from various walks of life. These included a nurse, a university lecturer, an actor, several union officials, and a physician."[23] In the perspective of Soviet and East German espionage habits, Carlos was, in the words of one historian, "indulged like a dignitary from the Soviet Kremlin."[24]

From his protected place within the embrace of the STASI, Carlos was able to continue with the institutional raids in Western Europe such as the ones that had begun his career. However, his previous penchant for bungled attacks reemerged. One such mission, which would have proven catastrophic had it not failed, was a rocket assault on a French nuclear plant, the *Superphenix,* located on the Rhone River near the border of Switzerland. Fortunately for the French, Carlos miscalculated his own firepower, and the rockets were unable to pierce the fortified walls. It has been alleged that one of his primary attorneys in later trials, Jacques Verges, participated in the attack himself.

---

[21] Rotten.com, Carlos the Jackal

[22] Colin Smith, Short Cuts, London Review of Books, Vol. 34 No. 2 – January 26, 2012, p.20

[23] Colin Smith, Short Cuts

[24] Colin Smith, Short Cuts

Verges

Despite Soviet and East German support, Carlos remained on the run living in Western Europe as the various missions unfolded. In 1976, as European authorities stepped up efforts to apprehend him for the murder of the two French agents and Moukharbal, he took refuge in Algiers rather than moving eastward toward his Soviet connections. Not as popular as he once had been, Carlos nevertheless was granted official asylum there.

Such protection became crucial that year because he involved himself with another spectacular action that would shake the world: the hijacking of an airliner with well over two hundred hostages in the name of the PFLP, a plan designed under the supervision of Haddad. Unfortunately for Carlos and the PFLP, it was not the hijacking that turned out to be so famous but the Israeli raid that rescued the great majority of the hostages and neutralized the terrorists as the plane sat on the tarmac at Entebbe Airport in Uganda. The non-Jews among the 248 captives were already set free, but when agents of the Mossad and combined elements of the Ugandan Army and Police stormed the plane in the middle of the night, the terrorists were killed. Three of the remaining hostages lost their lives, as did 45 Ugandan soldiers and Benjamin Netanyahu's older brother Yoni.

The psychological effect of the event had an opposite effect on the viewing worldwide public, and the raid of Entebbe is considered one of the greatest anti-terrorism missions conducted in the modern age. As an ideal of special ops work at the national and international level, it is widely studied by anti-terrorism agencies. For Carlos, the successful hijacking turned into a defeat in public perception, as Israel won the day, although little publicity followed for the heightened Ugandan casualties.

Wadie Haddad died in 1978, and that deprived Carlos of his first major employer and collaboration with anti-Israeli Palestinians. Some claim that he died of leukemia, but an outlying theory suggests that he was sent poisoned Belgian chocolates from a group allied with the KGB. Regardless, with him went a certain degree of the distrust between Carlos and the PFLP that came out of the OPEC raid. He became useful again for specific actions worked out between the Middle East and the Soviet Union. In addition to a few Middle Eastern countries, recruitment for his services increased in Soviet bloc states at a greater distance from Moscow, which never came to embrace him as fully as had the STASI or regional agencies. In the same year, Carlos added a new system of professional connections through a close association with Madeleine Kopp, a West German member of the Organization of Armed Arab Struggle. By the end of the 1970s, Carlos and Kopp began a courtship that would result in the two marrying some years later.

By 1980, Carlos' initial flamboyance and swagger returned. Although he had been a marked man by the CIA, the French Police, and Interpol for some years, his apparent belief that it was unnecessary for him to fade into the shadows gave rise to the hope that he could be more easily found and assassinated. The results did not fulfill expectations, however, as multiple CIA attempts to find and kill him failed.

Covering a great deal of ground in 1981, Carlos was reportedly spotted in numerous locations around the globe. In that year, a jubilant Mexican Police Force announced proudly that they had captured Carlos the Jackal, but the prisoner turned out to be only an armed robbery suspect with an eerie physical likeness to the terrorist.

That same year, Carlos initiated a series of attacks on such institutions as the offices of Radio Free Europe, clearly working on behalf of the Soviets. Again, his profile rose among anti-Western powers, and a concerted international pressure was directed against any nation that housed, hid, or supported his attacks in any way. However, despite their best efforts, Europe and the U.S. were not able to secure a consensus on driving Carlos out into the open. Almost immediately following the Radio Free Europe attacks, the Romanian Securitate hired him for the purpose of assassinating Romanian dissidents throughout France.

In April of 1982, he organized a car bombing in France that killed one and injured 63. The following month, still unable to track him down, authorities did the next best thing by arresting Madeleine Kopp, who was detained in the company of Swiss terrorist Bruno Breguet after their car was filled with explosives. Carlos turned to a series of threatened bombings and assassinations in order to secure her release, including one against the Mayor of Paris. When his demands went unmet and Kopp was incarcerated, he followed through on a great many of them. These included the bombing of a Beirut facility and a passenger train in France, killing five and wounding several. A few weeks after, he personally assassinated a French Embassy worker along with his pregnant wife in Lebanon. Similarly, he staged bombings at the French Embassy in Austria and a well-regarded restaurant in Paris that was a gathering place for French high society. He then went on to attack the Maison de France, a high society retail establishment associated with the Institute of French Culture in West Berlin, and in December of that year, two more French passenger trains were hit with powerful explosions under his direction.

Bruno Breguet

The Berlin attack added to an already growing sense of discomfort between Soviet espionage agencies, Carlos, and the STASI. The erratic motivations of certain attacks and a continued "lavish playboy"[25] lifestyle struck the Soviets as unprofessional, similar to how it had struck the Palestinians as immoral. No espionage agency in the world mastered or mandated internal secrecy more successfully than the KGB and its counterpart in East Germany, and Carlos' outgoing behavior represented far too loose an attitude toward the work to be done. His links with the KGB were already tenuous, and they requested that Carlos avoid any further attacks in Berlin while Soviet leader Leonid Brezhnev was visiting the city.

Although he obeyed the directive, within a few weeks the Soviet system began to lose control over Carlos' activities. The KGB all but severed ties with him, leaving him defenseless in the Eastern bloc states. East Germany, whose police force followed suit, cost Carlos dearly in every category of support his missions required. Being alienated from most of the active Palestinian groups as well, many of his safe houses around the East and Middle East were abruptly shut down, while many former accomplices and current connections withdrew their willingness to work with him.

---

[25] Michael Ray, Carlos the Jackal, Venezuelan Militant, Encyclopaedia Britannica – www.britannica.com/biography/Carlos-the-Jackal

Whether Carlos' attacks had any significant effect on Madeleine Kopp's ensuing trial is difficult to determine, Nevertheless she and members of her group were sentenced to six years in prison. Considering her status as a terrorist in her own right, and with her romantic connection to Carlos, the sentence seemed tame enough, and in the end, one year was eventually waived for good behavior, suggesting that the French had in some degree acceded to his threats.

Again, the West went after those nations that still harbored Carlos, sensing that his sphere of movement was shrinking drastically. In a more successful plan than to simply chase him through Europe and the Middle East, the change of emphasis to countries that furnished his supply lines enjoyed at least one success. Hungary, among the most stubborn of havens and rigidly held within the Soviet sphere for the better part of the century, expelled Carlos in 1985.

Despite that setback, Carlos married Madeleine Kopp in 1985, and a year later in 1986, daughter Elba Rose was born to the couple. In addition to Elba, Carlos had a son by an unnamed mother and two daughters from another woman.

Chapter 5: The End of Carlos the Jackal's Terror

Enjoying married life with a fellow terrorist on the run was an unworkable lifestyle, and Carlos went into forced retirement in Syria, staying there through the late 1980s. Syria was not an enthusiastic host, and it required that he curb his tendencies toward Western habits if he was to remain a welcome guest. In addition, he was ordered to "remain inactive"[26] as an operative in any country, and he was required to work if he was to stay within the graces of the Syrian government.

It seemed for a while that Carlos was obeying his instructions, despite a 20 day hunger strike in November of 1998, and in the view of agencies that had hunted him for years, he was no longer a current threat. Absent from the top of the priority list, Carlos was "virtually ignored"[27] by law enforcement through the remainder of the decade, which gave him some room for movement.

The fall of the Soviet communist structure came to mean many things to many people, but for Carlos the Jackal, it "spelled the end of his career"[28] in terms of any similarity to what it had once been. The KGB as an official government institution passed into history, even if its most illustrious members did not; as Vladimir Putin has demonstrated, many KGB agents reinvented themselves at the top of Russia's new power structure. Without the moorings of the KGB, the East German STASI was rendered similarly "unofficial" and unable to plan and carry out any significant actions. Once the Soviet side of the equation neutralized, collaborations with Middle Eastern factions, which already expressed little trust in Carlos, could not easily go forward.

---

[26] Murders and Mysteries, Carlos the Jackal

[27] Michael Ray, Carlos the Jackal

[28] Michael Ray, Carlos the Jackal

An American and European economic presence soon appeared in Russia, symbolizing the very threat that Carlos had labored to destroy, an unwelcome imperial reality in the epicenter of Marxist practice. In terms of personal safety, Carlos' vulnerability was maximized, and at the same time, his host country of Syria grew tired of his decadent lifestyle. At the turn of the 1990s, he converted to Islam, but whether this was intended in part to appease the Syrians and forestall the wearing out of his welcome is unknown.

When Kuwait was invaded by Iraq and rumors abounded that Saddam Hussein was recruiting Carlos to deal with specific enemies, it tested Syria's loyalty to him even further. Whether or not Carlos believed that his spiritual transformation would help to prolong his Syrian sponsorship, the time came when it no longer served the government to allow him to stay, so he made a hasty move to Sudan, where he lived under the protection of a fundamentalist Sheikh.

Returning to France for various actions, he claims to have married a Muslim woman in 1994 and purportedly smuggled her into France tied up in a sack. Many of the ensuing attacks in France were self-designed. Living two lives as a "militant and womanizing party animal,"[29] and at the same time, a successful jihadist attacking "anything Israeli or thought to be pro-Israeli,"[30] Carlos did his best to work without the full backing of the former support system. In many cases, the result signaled a return to an earlier amateurism that left him looking desperate and vulnerable.

Well aware of Islam's moral dictates, Carlos was, as before, unable to avoid offending his new host with his "playboy ways."[31] Openly continuing his regimen of wild sex and booze parties, in tandem with his newly adopted scriptures and marital status, both the Sheikh and the Sudanese government ran out of patience and at last handed him over to the French for trial. Unable to capture him for well over a decade, the French government was surprised to see Carlos deliver himself into their hands by dint of the consequences of his Bond-like self-image and Hollywood lifestyle.

The nature of Carlos' capture by the French in 1994 is the subject of an ongoing ethical and legal debate, and it has been both investigated and tried in court on more than one occasion. The question of whether the transfer from Sudan to France was legal, even under French law, is still up for official consideration. Some claim that in an unusual alternative to a traditional official extradition, Carlos was taken from his sickbed while recovering from testicular surgery in Khartoum. He had opted for the procedure due to concerns over a low sperm count. Others deny this story and claim that he was instead arrested on August 14 in the capital city traveling with a group of suspicious individuals, all bearing Arab passports. Carlos carried a false diplomatic passport, and the age of 44 was the only statistic listed on the document that was deemed

---

[29] Whiskey Online, Carlos the Jackal: Timeline for a Drunken Terrorist, Social Revolutionary, June 29, 2011 – www.whiskeyonline.com
[30] Whiskey Online, Carlos the Jackal
[31] Rotten.com, Carlos the Jackal

legitimate. It was this dubious passport, according to the French, that had caused him to be held under surveillance in the first place. A third claim suggests that he was arrested during a liposuction procedure, by which Carlos hoped to "remove fat from his waist."[32]

France and Sudan shared no extradition treaty, and yet French officials were permitted to take Carlos from Sudanese soil without legal recourse. Most accounts agree with the suggestion that the French agents virtually "sedated and kidnapped"[33] Carlos in an elaborate sting worked out by several factions in both the West and East. Following the abduction, he was smuggled out of the city in secrecy and, more than likely, in a state of unconsciousness.

Historians and biographers generally categorize the arrest as more of a surreptitious abduction, and they find interesting parallels in the fact that it occurred in tandem with high-level diplomatic visits between the two countries. Burr and Collins, in an exhaustive analysis of recent Sudanese history, make note of the most important one. They claim in *Sudan in Turmoil: Hassan al-Turabi and the Islamist State* that it was "no accident that the French abduction…occurred shortly after a diplomatic visit to France"[34] by Hassan al-Turabi of the National Islamic Front, later called the National Congress. Despite French claims of an honest arrest within the laws of the host country, Burr and Collins believe that the evidence points to "the world's most elusive criminal"[35] being secretly pilfered in the middle of the night in a semi-conscious state. It is theorized that Sudan assisted in the transfer of Carlos back to France as a way of being removed from the list of terrorist countries by the United States, and it is known that both France and the U.S. talked secretly with Sudan, offering various deals for his transfer.

---

[32] Los Angeles Times, August 21, 1994, Reuters, Carlos the Jackal Arrested During Liposuction – www.articles.latimes.org/1994-05-21/news/mn-29612_1_carlos-the-jackal

[33] The Seattle Times – Carlos the Jackal Captured in Sudan – linked to '72 Munich massacre, other attacks over 2 decades – www.community.seattletimes.nwsource.com/archive/?date=19940815+slug=1925369

[34] Lidwien Kapteijns, Review of Sudan in Turmoil: Hasan al-Turabi (Sudan) and the Islamist State, 1899-2003, by J. Millard Burr, Robert O. Collins, International Journal of African Historical Studies, Vol. 43 No. 2 (2010), p. 394

[35] BBC News, World, Carlos the Jackal – three decades of crime – www.news.bbc.co.uk/1/hi/42244.stm

Al-Turabi

Almost immediately upon hearing of the capture, Austria sued for its share of the prisoner, seeking to try him for the murders incurred in the OPEC raid and other actions, in addition to charges of kidnapping and trespass. In order to accomplish such an extradition from a French government that was holding on tight to its long-time prey, it was beneficial for Austria to share the view that the French were not fully entitled to have taken Carlos in such a manner.

The most impassioned defender among Carlos' family members, brother Vladimir, has expressed a belief that France is in the process of sending Carlos to Austria as soon as they can find a method by which they would save face, having failed for so long to capture an international criminal living in their own capital city. According to Vladimir, what he describes as a willingness to hand Carlos over to the Austrians is based on their knowledge that they are in "a weak legal position."[36] Whether he was correct in such an assumption, or whether dynamics changed within the two governments, such a transfer was not made or publicly discussed.

Carlos' first appearance in a French court caused a press sensation around the world, and the frenzy was all the more enhanced by his wild courtroom antics, including outbursts and salutes of solidarity to his fellow terrorists. According to one biographer, the trial had "all the profile of a captured yeti,"[37] and suggested that the international press could not have been more excited "as they must have been at [the trial of] Mata Hari…"[38] At the onset, Carlos was asked to relate to the court the precise nature of his profession, to which he replied, "Professional revolutionary in the Leninist tradition."[39]

[36] Alex Bellos, World News, The Guardian, A Call for Jackal's Freedom, 30 May, 1999 – www.theguardian.com/world/1999/may/31/alexbellos
[37] Colin Smith, Short Cuts
[38] Colin Smith, Short Cuts
[39] John Henley, World News, The Guardian, Carlos the Jackal to Wed his Lawyer, Oct. 12, 2001 –

Attorneys for the defense made a concerted effort at the onset by attempting to dispel the notion that Carlos was an insensate murderer and mercenary who took a perverse pleasure at the results of his violence. He testified that in all of his actions, he "tried to do it cold…[in the] least painful way possible."[40] He added, "I'm not a sadist or a masochist – I don't enjoy the suffering of others."[41] Asked how he could justify the deaths and injuries to so many, he likened his struggles to nations at war: "When one makes war for over 30 years, there is a lot of blood spilled – mine and others – but we never killed anyone for money, but for a cause – the liberation of Palestine."[42]

In the end, the French could not have possibly acquitted Carlos after spending two decades attempting to apprehend him. In a surprise statement, he denied the killing of the two agents and Michel Moukharbal in 1975, claiming instead that the executions were orchestrated by the Mossad, the most important and federally connected of a handful of Israeli secret services. Regardless, he was convicted and sentenced to life in prison, as expected. In a final signal to the world press and fellow revolutionaries, Carlos "raised a defiant fist as he was led away to the cells."[43] The prosecutor's response to the proceedings were succinct – "He [Carlos] hasn't learned a thing or forgotten a thing."[44] Having first been incarcerated at La Santé, Carlos was to be relocated at a later date to Clairvaux Prison for the duration of his sentence.

www.theguardian.com/world/2001/oct/13/johnhenley

[40] Free Republic, Carlos the Jackal Sneers at Al Qaeda's 'amateur' Killers – July 15, 2007 – www.freerepublic.com/focus/f-news/1866755/posts

[41] Rotten.com, Carlos the Jackal

[42] Crime Magazine, December 12, 2012, Carlos the Jackal and the OPEC Attack - 1975

[43] CNN, Carlos the Jackal on trial for 1985 bombings in France – Vol. 7, 2011 – www.cnn.com/2011/11/07/world/europe/france-carlos-the-jackal-grial/index.html.

[44] CNN, Carlos the Jackal

Michael C. Berch's picture of La Santé Prison in Paris

Clairvaux
Prison

In 1997, Carlos reappeared in court on a second set of charges, which included a series of bombings from 20 years prior. In the second trial, the defense was passionately handled by Isabelle Coutant-Peyre, a defense attorney who had served as a junior member at the 1994 trial. She immediately served notice to the press and the court that her client, now 51 years of age, was in a "fighting mood."[45] She further claimed that Carlos had not been implicated in any of the assaults by any tangible evidence, and that he was present as "a scapegoat and victim of an accumulated myth." Further, she expressed her conviction to the court that "a great lie is being prepared,"[46] based on nothing more than a concocted persona by a government who needed to avoid humiliating itself further.

A more subdued Carlos sat through the proceedings in 1997 as the outer world's interest waned, moving on to other crises and other high-profile figures in the news. In a comparison of coverage from the first trial, the 1997 proceedings were described by one individual in attendance as "skimpy."[47] Coutant-Peyre was able to have Carlos released from solitary confinement, but his conviction from the first trial was upheld, and a second life sentence was imposed for the second conviction, to be served at Clairvaux.

[45] John Henley, World News, the Guardian
[46] Colin Smith, Short Cuts
[47] Colin Smith, Short Cuts

Venezuela was in an indignant uproar as the trial began, as they had been since Carlos' capture three years prior. Hugo Chavez, beginning his first term as the Venezuelan President, hailed Carlos as a national hero, a "distinguished compatriot,"[48] and forwarded a letter of solidarity to his fellow revolutionary through diplomatic channels. In it, he referred to his countryman not as a terrorist but as a "revolutionary fighter,"[49] and declared that the foreign ministry would be urged to "investigate allegations"[50] of kidnapping on the part of France. Such an investigation was eventually pursued, although the inevitable decision was not to Chavez' liking. Addressing whether he could support Carlos' actions in good conscience, the Venezuelan president added in his manifesto, "There is a time to gather stones, and to cast them away – a time to ignite the revolution, or ignore it."[51] Chavez remained through the years among the most vocal supporters of Carlos' innocence, and he continued to speak as one of the fiercest critics of his countryman's treatment at the hands of the French government.

---

[48] Alex Bellos, The Guardian
[49] Murders and Mysteries, Carlos the Jackal
[50] Alex Bellos, The Guardian
[51] Colin Smith, Short Cuts

Hugo Chavez

Carlos and Coutant-Peyre began a courtship in 1997, the year of the second trial, and were married in 2001. It was Carlos' third marriage, and little is known of what became of his previous relationships to Kopp and al Jarrar, his Muslim wife. Coutant-Peyre had recently separated from her husband. In an explanation of her attraction to a convicted terrorist, Coutant-Peyre responded that their relationship was "a marriage of love and compatibility of ideas."[52] However, in a less ideologically-driven statement, she later confessed to being drawn in and charmed by his "courtly Spanish ways,"[53] echoing similar statements made by Madeleine Kopp. Carlos and Coutant-Peyre were married in a prison office in what Carlos described as "a form of Muslim marriage."[54]

---

[52] John Henley, World News, the Guardian
[53] Colin Smith, Short Cuts

Chapter 6: Prison

Incarcerated for almost a decade in Clairvaux, Carlos occupied much of his time organizing the fine points of his ideology and the precious few memoirs he could safely reveal for a book entitled *L'Islam Revolutionnaire* (Islamic Revolution), which he released in June of 2003 with *Editions du Roche*. It was written under the supervision of Jean-Michel Vernochet, an author for Figaro in Paris and a professor at one of the city's schools of journalism. The book was scant on personal memories, as the French were quick to pounce on any new information that could be used in court. It has been described, rather, as a "defense and illustration"[55] of terrorism.

Many have questioned how the book ever came to light, as rules concerning correspondence from French prisons would generally prevent such a large project from coming out. Vernochet states that in his collaboration with Carlos, the two never met, and that he assembled the text through letters, interviews, and texts forwarded from Carlos. The bulk of the text was presumably written outside of the prison.

In the text of *L'Islam Revolutionnaire,* Carlos hailed Osama bin Laden and called his terrorism a "shining"[56] example of the revolution's answer to the menace of "U.S. totalitarianism."[57] Commenting on the 9/11 attacks, he termed them a "lofty feat of arms"[58] and a major blow in the fight for equal wealth distribution worldwide. For the North American audience in particular, he added the warning that the attack was only the first step, and that "from now on, terrorism will be more or less a daily part of your rotting democracies."[59]

---

[54] John Henley, World News, the Guardian
[55] BBC News, Jackal Book Praises bin Laden, Thursday, 26 June, 2003 – www.news.bbc.co.uk/2/hi/302358.stm
[56] BBC News
[57] BBC News
[58] BBC News
[59] BBC News

Bin Laden

With Carlos safely in prison, his loose-knit organization was still considered a danger, and it continued to operate with a successful aura of secrecy. In 2004, following the notorious bombings in Madrid, a Spanish reporter did the unthinkable by infiltrating Carlos' inner circle at great personal risk. Antonio Salar, digesting a tremendous cache of information concerning the Palestinian struggle, and constructing a thorough personal biography, was able to interact with Carlos' colleagues and converse on a regular basis with Carlos himself. Salar was passed off as Mohammad Abdulah, a radical Islamist, and even underwent circumcision to complete the picture. The concocted story of his family tree included Palestinian grandparents, although he claimed to be Venezuelan and Spanish. Through time, he became the personal webmaster for Carlos, which required frequent phone conversations between the two men. The first came about by accident, as Carlos called his family while Salar was visiting with them. Put on the phone in impromptu fashion, they spoke in Arabic and Spanish for a time. Salar apparently passed inspection at the onset.

This regimen of contact, however, was for Salar particularly nerve-racking, as he found Carlos to be unusually astute and sensitive to the subtleties of speech and intimate knowledge of the revolution's inner workings. Salar observed later that he was "worried about my security,"[60] and was relieved to be released from an invitation to meet with Carlos personally at La Santé Prison, fearing that his cover could be too easily blown. Many of his interactions were accomplished with hidden cameras after the Madrid bombings, but despite a faithful adherence to his mission,

---

[60] World News, The Guardian, October 10, 2010, Carlos the Jackal Was My Friend – www.theguardian.com/world/2010/oct/10/carlos-the-jackal-was-my-friend

Salar developed some degree of empathy for Carlos, and was both unsettled and moved by the prisoner's "strange offer of friendship."[61]

Always eager to reach the public after the fall of his adventurous career, Carlos participated in a television documentary in 2004, during which he was interviewed at length. He spoke freely and with great frankness. The comments that found their way to the final cut of the documentary, however, backfired on him in a legal sense. The French court brought additional charges of terrorism as a result of the documentary's release. Three years later, Carlos won his appeal when the court agreed that his comments had been taken out of context. For his trouble, he was awarded 5,000 Euros.

He was not, however, to get away unscathed. In 2007, French judge Jean-Louis Bruguiere brought additional charges against him related to numerous bombings carried out by Carlos in the early 80s. In its initial indecision as to which crimes to prosecute, the French justice system decided to prosecute small groups of charges at regular intervals, which kept Carlos in court on a constant basis. The magistrate, Bruguiere, was a tough-minded expert on terrorism, and had grown up in the ranks of the police in actual pursuit of specific criminals. In 2004, he was named Vice-President of the Paris Court of Serious Claims, and pursued terrorists who violated French law despite surviving multiple attacks on his residence, including one grenade attack. It was Bruguiere, who did much of the legwork in making sure that Carlos was apprehended in Sudan, and it is generally assumed that the capture would not have happened without the magistrate's contribution.

---

[61] World News, The Guardian

Bruguiere

2007 continued to be an interesting one for Carlos, as his former wife, photographer and fellow terrorist Madeleine Kopp released a tell-all book about her time with the notorious terrorist. In the salacious memoir of two revolutionaries on the run, she describes their initial meeting, during which she found Carlos to be exceedingly unattractive with his "round baby face, parted short hair and suit and tie."[62] She recalls that at the time that he looked like some type of "creepy

[62] Tony Patterson, Berlin, The Telegraph, Carlos the Jackal's Wife Launches Tell-All Book, Sept. 2, 1907 – www.telegraph/co/uk/news/worldnews/1661978/carlos-the-jackals-wife-launches-tell-all-book.htm

conformist."[63] Within a brief period, he began making sexual advances toward Kopp, who at first found him repellent, and he apparently did himself no favors by nicknaming her "the cow."[64] However, Kopp admitted that after continued contact with Carlos, she found herself "unable to resist him,"[65] despite having full knowledge of the "notoriety and danger that came with it."[66] Carlos and Kopp remained together for 13 years, and by the time they were married, the assessment of her husband had changed considerably, as expressed in the memoirs:"[When you are] seduced by such a man, you get seduced and simply obey."[67] She was equally captivated by his ideological thoughts, which she found to be strangely poetic, and she asserted that he had a gift for making women feel as though they were an indispensable part of the struggle, "the other half of the coming revolution."[68]

In 2010, movie director Olivier Assayas released a miniseries film of almost six hours in length on the story of Carlos the Jackal, titled simply *Carlos*. While the film was of interest in the U.S. and other Western countries, it was a sensation in South America, communist strongholds in general, and parts of Europe. According to the critics, *Carlos* was a triumph, with one critic declaring the casting as "perfect"[69] and perhaps too easily assuming that it employed "good historical accuracy, as far as anyone knows."[70] However, according to one historian viewing the film, the major flaw is that it "makes you love him, despite being a shallow demagogue…Marxist turned Islamist…gun for hire."[71]

Carlos himself was furious upon seeing the film, and he flatly declared that he hated it. Rather than furthering the Palestinian cause, or at least shedding light on the issues with Israel, Assayas, according to Carlos, set out only to make money through the sensationalist depiction of a stereotype entirely ungrounded in reality. Further, he did this without any care for accuracy, and with no sympathy for the real life struggles which Carlos and the Palestinian people had undergone. This, to Carlos, was no mere instance of artistic license but a "dirty and deliberate fabrication of the facts…pure, unadulterated bad faith."[72]

Understandably, much of Carlos' ire is reserved for the way in which the title character was portrayed, with a script that created "one long caricature from beginning to end."[73] According to the film, Carlos spent a good deal of his time high on drugs, which he claims to have never done.

---

[63] Tony Patterson, The Telegraph

[64] Tony Patterson, The Telegraph

[65] Tony Patterson, The Telegraph

[66] Tony Patterson, The Telegraph

[67] Tony Patterson, The Telegraph

[68] Tony Patterson, The Telegraph

[69] Hussain Abdul Hussain, Huffington Post, The Blog, Movie Review: Carlos – www.huffingtonpost.com/hussain-abdulhussain/movie-review-carlos_b_763206.html

[70] Hussain Abdul Hussain, Huffington Post

[71] Hussain Abdul Hussain, Huffington Post

[72] Colin Smith, Short Cuts

[73] Colin Smith, Short Cuts

Scenes where the character sprays the air with ammunition portrayed the real revolutionary, according to Carlos, as an idiotic amateur. Similarly, he was incensed with the way he was portrayed as "treating women like dogs."[74] He greatly objected to the film's suggestion that Saddam Hussein recognized him as an important figure and made secret advances to him for work as an assassin. Carlos is insistent that Hussein "never recognized our organization."[75] The charge of being a mercenary was old news for Carlos, but the film's insistence on him building a personal fortune through swindling and playing off one faction against another aroused a fierce response: "If I was one (a mercenary), why didn't I take the offer from the CIA to work for them?"[76] Finally, he was livid at the depiction of his former wife, Madeleine Kopp, as both a whore and an agent for the East German STASI, neither of which, he claims, is or ever was true.

In November of 2011, Carlos was brought forward for yet another trial, and a month later, was found guilty of another 11 deaths from many years prior. On December 15th, he stood to be sentenced, largely a moot point given the breadth of past sentences. The court asked the defendant if he had anything to say, which was its duty. Carlos "nodded and took five hours to say it."[77] The judge took no liberties with the law and protected Carlos' right to speak, regardless of duration, before an exhausted court. For 17 years, he had been in or around French prisons, and by now spoke the language brilliantly.

In a sense, he began to filibuster the assembly in one of his many fluent tongues. He began with rhetorical apologies to the court by saying, "Excuse me for taking my time, but I'm a living archive, and most people at my level are dead."[78] His marathon speech alternated between nostalgia and a recounting of his most deeply-held revolutionary principles. Citing leaders and fellow terrorists around the world as important to the much-needed revolution, he paid tribute to Osama bin Laden as a new force in the anti-West struggle. He extolled the domestic triumph of Romania's Nicolae Ceausescu, who, in Carlos' words, "wiped out Romania's terrible debt"[79] by paying off all of the country's foreign debt and passing a law prohibiting further exterior loans. When he came to the name of Gaddafi, however, he broke down and sobbed, referring to the Libyan leader as "a giant among men."[80] When at last he completed his remarks, the sentencing commenced, providing for Carlos to receive parole at the age of 80, a useless exercise considering the previous life sentences.

---

[74] Colin Smith, Short Cuts
[75] Colin Smith, Short Cuts
[76] Colin Smith, Short Cuts
[77] Colin Smith, Short Cuts
[78] Colin Smith, Short Cuts
[79] Colin Smith, Short Cuts
[80] Colin Smith, Short Cuts

Ceausescu

The absence of good fortune with French courts continued through June 26 of 2013, when the Court of Appeals upheld his life sentence for the four bombings in France. That same year, he lost one of his greatest supporters, both materially and psychologically, with the passing of Venezuelan President Hugo Chavez in his home country.

With a new generation of terrorists making headlines, especially bin Laden, Carlos the Jackal passed out of the lexicon of top anti-imperialist operatives, and he keenly felt the disappearance of his former notoriety. What was once the "young man standing on the runway wearing sunglasses, a black Che Guevara beret and a Pierre Cardin leather jacket"[81] had now aged significantly, was overweight, and suffered from diabetes. Yet, in the captivity of a French prison, he still spoke as an international person by claiming that "the world is my domain,"[82] with a suggestion that if there was a place he could not reach, one of his people certainly could. In a real sense, the statement was true, as his organization survived, maintained by both former and younger colleagues.

The French justice system has continued to charge Carlos in piecemeal fashion, every few months bringing a new set of charges for a specific set of events. On October 7 of 2014, he was again brought before the judge for a series of grenade attacks committed in Paris. The guilty verdict seemed all but inevitable, and the sentencing all but academic after so many such trials.

From the beginning of the prison sentence first handed down in 1994, Carlos has complained of what he regards as his inhumane and degrading treatment in the facility. However, photos leaked to the public told quite another story. A deal with French authorities appeared to be in the offing, for once out of solitary confinement, Carlos was abruptly placed in an "opulent living space"[83] consisting of a "fully furnished suite,"[84] replete with "hotel quality amenities."[85] The public further learned that Carlos had free access to radio, television, and the internet. Limits on the range of Internet accessibility were unknown, but the French citizenry seemed particularly incensed by his luxurious living conditions.

Major biographers, such as David Wallop, have taken up the idea that Carlos the Jackal and much of his life as a terrorist and agent for anti-Israeli and anti-capitalist attacks is, indeed, a myth, as has been suggested by others. Wallop insists that the hype surrounding Carlos' exploits is entirely in error, despite the fact that he is guilty of multiple murders. He does not, says Wallop, in the least resemble the "sleek, icily efficient, glamorous super-terrorist"[86] that the press and the public imagination have made him out to be. In actuality, as suggested in Wallop's book, *The Search for the World's Most Wanted Man, The Question of Carlos,* Carlos was "a bungler, a poor shot, and a coward."[87] Wallop further suggests that where Carlos may have been involved in masterminding certain actions and events, he was at best "an armchair revolutionary,"[88] while others were more authentically devoted to the cause, more willing to face danger, and less desirous of fame, comfort, and public image. Much of this fantasy Wallop lays at the feet of the

---

[81] CNN, Carlos the Jackal on Trial

[82] CNN, Carlos the Jackal on Trial

[83] NNDB, Carlos the Jackal – www.nndb.com/people/317/000050167/

[84] NNDB, Carlos the Jackal

[85] NNDB, Carlos the Jackal

[86] The New York Times, David Wallop, The Search for the World's Most Wanted Man, Review, The Question of Carlos, January, 1994, Random House, NY – www.nytimes.com/1994/01/02/books/the-question-of-carlos.html

[87] The New York Times, David Wallop

[88] The New York Times, David Wallop

French, who put forth "a myth created to cover [their] embarrassing inability to snare the terrorist."[89] It is likely, he suggests, that nobody will ever know precisely which actions came under Carlos's auspices, or his specific role in any, as he has confused the search by wrongly claiming involvement in some and creating many others in the public imagination that never existed.

In other assertions, Wallop feels certain that it was Saddam Hussein, not Gaddafi, who recruited and instructed Carlos through the entire OPEC raid. He suggests as well that the KGB played a much important role in several of the actions than is known, and although they once considered Carlos for recruitment, they were put off by his personal failings and abandoned the idea of employing him. Ironically, Wallop also believes that in the end, it was the KGB who betrayed Carlos, and in hindsight, the imprisoned terrorist seems to agree by stating that "the KGB stabbed me in the back."[90] In terms of his abduction from Sudan, Carlos acknowledges many dealings behind the scene, but in the end, he claimed, "I wasn't arrested. I was sold by the Sudanese government."[91]

Carlos has also asserted in both interviews and court testimony that the presence of states behind terrorist actions, no matter how anonymously, is a given, and that there is truly no such thing as the lone terrorist acting out a personal quest outside of the movies. In effect, "all terrorism is state terrorism."[92] The terrorist remains the pawn of the state and of the changing relationships between governments, secret agencies and their counterparts. A terrorist, then, is only effective when he is in favor with his national sponsor.

In his rigorous court testimony, which defended his actions and the revolution in general, Carlos may have been obliged to salute iconic terrorists who came after him, but his personal opinions concerning the rise of al-Qaeda and Osama bin Laden are not entirely positive. In bin Laden's case, sources say that Carlos' ego took a hit because the man behind 9/11 "stole his crown"[93] as the era's most notorious terrorist. Obviously, the event, especially for the U.S., trumped anything Carlos had done in terms of human life, property, and shock value. As for al-Qaeda activities around the world, he bemoans the decision to target ordinary people, particularly in Great Britain. He claimed to be "saddened"[94] by the ensuing loss of life in the city of London, and he has accused al-Qaeda of a general "lack of professionalism."[95]

In a belief that it is bin Laden who should have received such a hideous nickname, Carlos still views the term "Jackal" as an irritant. Although the fact is not known worldwide, "Jackal" is also

---

[89] The New York Times, David Wallop

[90] Colin Smith, Short Cuts

[91] Colin Smith, Short Cuts

[92] Colin Smith, Short Cuts

[93] Free Republic, Carlos the Jackal Sneers at Al-Qaeda's 'amateur' killers, July 15, 2007 – www.freerepublic.com/focus/f-news/1866755/posts/

[94] Free Republic

[95] Free Republic

the nickname given to an unpopular police chief in Venezuela.

While Carlos' wife, Coutant-Peyre, continues to lobby for his release and complains of a future with no traditional marriage, Carlos is the more philosophical of the two, remarking, "Things are more difficult for her than me, but this is the price to pay for one's struggle against the empire."[96]

Among the many studies of the terrorist mind, the world of psychology is for the most part agreed on the idea that in order for one to seek out such a life, a "narcissistic personality disorder"[97] is prerequisite. According to the prevailing theory, some initial damage to the self-esteem must have been suffered early on, and the thrill of terrorist actions provides what the field calls "psychodynamic rewards"[98] in order to compensate for such damage. This, according to popular thought, is why terrorists are so often "sensitive to public image and reputation."[99] Researcher and author Richard M. Pearlstein disagrees, claiming that Carlos serves as proof that narcissism is not required, and that he has "exhibited no such narcissistic disorders."[100] Others respond that Carlos is indeed highly sensitive to "public image and reputation" and enjoys serving as a model in motion pictures and novels by such authors as Tom Clancy and Robert Ludlum, not to mention the Bond-like fantasy in which he lived during the early years. Such passions, they argue, do represent a narcissistic state.

In reference, perhaps, to his early roots in the Catholic Church through the influence of his mother, Carlos has mellowed to some small degree on the matter of religion. Through his father, he wryly observed, "I was brought up as an atheist, but [I have] walked away from so many shootings [that I] began to think, 'Why am I here?'"[101] Still unrepentant, however, over his life and "work," the historical figures he most admires include Alexander the Great and Libya's Gaddafi. Derisive as ever toward Western ideals, social structures and cultural habits, Carlos' best hopes for the revolution are placed in modern-day Persia, and he remains convinced that "fundamentalist Iran is the new wave of anti-imperialism."[102]

Online Resources

Other 20th century history titles by Charles River Editors

Other titles about Carlos the Jackal on Amazon

---

[96] Free Republic
[97] Colin Smith, Short Cuts
[98] Colin Smith, Short Cuts
[99] Colin Smith, Short Cuts
[100] Colin Smith, Short Cuts
[101] Free Republic
[102] Los Angeles Times, , Reuters

Bibliography

About News – Carlos the Jackal – Profile of Carlos the Jackal –
www.terrorism.about.com/od/groupsleader/p/CarlostheJackal.htm

Baader-Meinhof.com – the Baader-Meinhof Gang and the Invention of Modern Terrorism –
www.baader-meinhof.com/tag/carlos-the-jackal./

BBC News, World, Carlos the Jackal-three decades of crime-
www.news.bbc.co.uk/2/hi/42244.stm

BBC News, Jackal Book Praises bin Laden, Thursday, 26 June, 2003 –
www.bbcnews.co.uk/2/hi/302358.stm

Bellos, Alex, Comp Call for Jackal's Freedom – World News, The Guardian, 30 May, 1999 –
www.theguardian.com/world/1999/may/31/alexbellos

CNN, Carlos the Jackal Fast Facts, CNN Library, Oct. 9, 2014 –
www.com/2013/04/26/world/americas/carlos-the-jackal-fast-facts/index.html

CNN, Carlos the Jackal on Trial for 1985 Bombings in France – Nov. 7, 2011 –
www.cnn.com/2011/11/07/world/europe/france-carlos-the-jackal-trial/index.html

Crime Magazine – Dec. 12, 2012 – Carlos the Jackal and the OPEC Attack - 1975

Dirges, Manohla, The New York Times, Oct., 2010 – The Days, Nights, and Years of the
Jackal: The Tale of a Terrorist – www.nytimes.com/2010/10/15/15carlos.html?_r_=0

FAS, Intelligence Resource Program – Japanese Red Army, Imperialist International Brigade
(AIIB) – www.fas.org/irp/world/para/htm

Free Republic, Carlos the Jackal Sneers at Al-Qaeda's 'Amateur' Killers – July 15, 2007 –
www.freerepublic.com/focus/f-news/18667551/posts

Germani, Clara, The Baltimore Sun, November 5, 1995 – www.articles-
baltimoresun.com/1995-11-05/news/1995309007_1_-patricia-lumumbia-dream-school-moscow

Hinnant, Lori/Greg Keller, Yahoo News – www.yahoo.com/carlos-the-jackal-ex-enigma-now-
mired-court-11108169.htm

History of War, Ilich Ramirez Sanchez (Carlos the Jackal), 1949 –
www.historyofwar.org./articles/people_jackal.html

Henley, John, World News, The Guardian, Oct. 12, 2001 – Carlos the Jackal to Wed His

Lawyer – www.theguardian.com/world/2001/oct/13/jonhen

History.com – The Terrorist Known as Carlos the Jackal is Captured, 1994 – www.history.com/this-day-in-history/the-terrorist-known-as-Carlos-the-Jackal-is-captured

Hussain, Abdul-Hussain, The Blog, Movie Review: Carlos – www.huffingtonpost.com/hussain-abdul-hussain/movie/review-carlos_b_763206.html

Jewish Virtual Library – Munich Olympic Massacre: Background and Overview – www.Jewishvirtuallibrary.org/source/terrorism/munich.html

Kapteijns, Lidwien, Review, Sudan in Turmoil: Hasan al-Turabi and the Islamist State, 1989-2003, J. Millard , Robert O. Collins, International Journal of African Historical Studies, Vol. 43 No. 2 (2010)

Los Angeles Times, August 21, 1994-08-21, Reuters: Carlos the Jackal Arrested During Liposuction – www.articles.latimes.org/1994-08-21/news/mn-29612_1_carlos-the-jackal

Low, Valentine – House Where Carlos the Jackal Struck Faces the Bulldozer – www.questia.com/newspaper/.GI-174665254.house-where-carlos-the-jackl-struck-faces-the-bulldozer

Murders and Mysteries, Carlos the Jackal – www.mysteriesandmurders.blogspot.com/2011/07/carlos-the-jackal.html

NNDB, Carlos the Jackal – www.nndb.com/people/317/000050167/

Patterson, Tony, Berlin, The Telegraph – Carlos the Jackal's Wife Launches Tell-All Book, Sept. 2, 2007 – www.telegraph.co.uk/news/worldnews/1561978/carlos-the-jackal-wife-launches-tell-all-book.htm

Ray, Michael, Carlos the Jackal, Venezuelan Militant – www.britannica.com/EncyclopaediaBritannica/Biography/Carlos-the-Jackal

Rotten.com – Carlos the Jackal – www.rotten.com/library/bio/crime/terrorists/carlos-the-jackal/

Smith, Colin, Short Cuts, London Review of Books, Vol. 34 No. 2 – January 26, 2012,

The Guardian, Tuesday, July 8, 1975, Carlos the Jackal is in London – www.theguardian.com/us-news/2015/jul/08/carlos-the-jackal-in-London-1975

The Seattle Times, Carlos the Jackal Captured in Sudan – Linked to '72 Munich Massacre, Other Attacks Over 2 Decades –

www.community.seattletimes.nwsource.com/archive/?date=199440815+slug=1925369

Wallop, David, The Search for Carlos, the World's Most Wanted Man, Review of The New York Times, Jan. 2, 1994, The Question of Carlos, Random House, New York City – www.nytimes.com/1994/01/02/books/the-question-of-Carlos.html

Whiskeyonline.com, June 9, 2011 – Carlos the Jackal: Timeline for a Drunken Terrorist, Social Revolutionary – www.whiskeyonline.com

World News, The Guardian, Oct. 10, 2010 – Carlos the Jackal Was My Friend – www.theguardian.com/world/2010/Oct/10/carlos-the-jackal-was-my-friend

Made in the USA
Las Vegas, NV
11 January 2022

40891931R00026